BRANCH LINES TO HARWICH AND HADLEIGH

Vic Mitchell

MP Middleton Press

Published June 2011

ISBN 978 1 908174 02 4

© Middleton Press, 2011

Design Deborah Esher

Published by
        Middleton Press
        Easebourne Lane
        Midhurst
        West Sussex
        GU29 9AZ
Tel: 01730 813169
Fax: 01730 812601
Email: info@middletonpress.co.uk
www.middletonpress.co.uk

Printed in the United Kingdom by Henry Ling Limited, at the Dorset Press, Dorchester, DT1 1HD

CONTENTS

INDEX

ACKNOWLEDGEMENTS

I am very grateful for the assistance received from many of those mentioned in the credits, also to A.R.Carder, G.Croughton, A.G.W.Garraway, S.C.Jenkins, G.Kenworthy, N.Langridge, B.Lewis, C.Phillips, Mr D. and Dr S.Salter and, in particular, my wife who has meticulously typeset my scribblings for 30 years. Included in my appreciation is Chris Cock who has kindly supplied data from the Bryan Wilson Signalling Register.

Ia. Railway Clearing House map from about 1930.

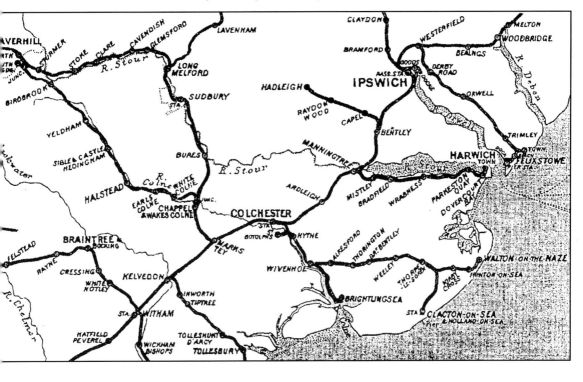

GEOGRAPHICAL SETTING

Harwich Branch

This is entirely in Essex, close to the southern shore of the tidal part of the River Stour. This was an ideal haven for shipping and extensive quays and docks developed over time, notably the Port of Harwich.

The line passes over only a few minor watercourses and the ground rises inland to a little over 100ft, thus only minimal earthworks were necessary.

Hadleigh Branch

The route has some notable cuttings near its west end, where it reaches around 200ft above sea level. Hadleigh developed as an important commercial centre and is immediately east of the small River Brett, which flows into the River Stour, five miles south of the town. The branch was close to the southern boundary of the county of Suffolk.

The maps are to the scale of 25ins to 1 mile with north at the top, unless otherwise indicated.

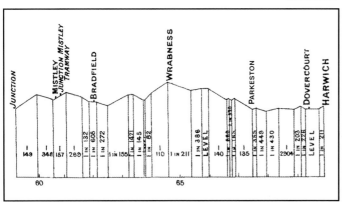
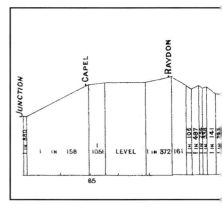

Ib. The 1956 edition at 2ins to 1 mile indicates the extent of the Parkeston development and the alignment of the original route. The GER built 32 cottages initially.

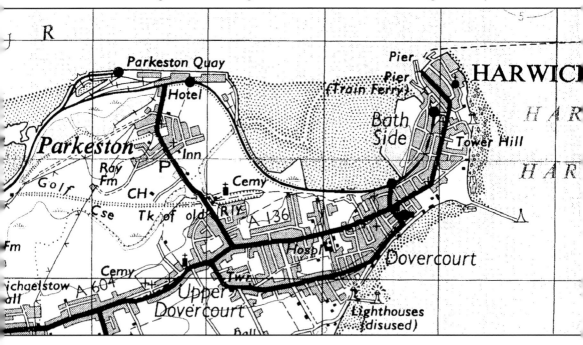

HISTORICAL BACKGROUND

Harwich Branch

Building of the Harwich Pier started in 1851 and it was opened by a local company in July 1853. The Eastern Union Railway's Act of 1842 resulted in a service between Colchester and Ipswich from 15th June 1846. This company opened its branch to Harwich Town on 15th August 1854 and became a constituent of the Great Eastern Railway upon its formation in 1862. A less direct route to Harwich via Parkeston Quay came into use in 1882 and the development of a massive port began. The original line lasted until 15th March 1883. The line east of Mistley was doubled at this time.

The GER became part of the London & North Eastern Railway in 1923 and this formed much of the Eastern Region of British Railways upon nationalisation in 1948.

The lines became part of Network SouthEast on 10th June 1986. Privatisation resulted in the routes being branded First Great Eastern on 5th January 1997, when FirstBus was awarded a 7 ¼ year franchise. This became First Group, but the operation was transferred to National Express, which applied the meaningless name of 'one' from 1st April 2004. It was rebranded National Express East Anglia in 2008. The "Mayflower Line" was used as a brand name for the branch from 1997.

Electrification - Regular services used 25kV AC from the outset. Colchester - Ipswich started on 13th May 1985, Manningtree - Harwich Town on 12th May 1986 and Ipswich - Norwich on 11th May 1987.

Hadleigh Branch

An Act dated 18th June 1846 provided for the Eastern Union & Hadleigh Junction Railway, which opened on 20th August 1847. The single line branch was leased to the Eastern Union Railway initially and purchased by it on 20th October 1847. The Eastern Counties Railway took over operation on 1st January 1854 and the GER did so on 7th August 1862. A triangular junction made direct running to Ipswich possible until 1875.

Closure to passenger traffic took place on 29th February 1932 and freight ceased on 16th April 1965.

PASSENGER SERVICES

Harwich Branch

The table below gives an indication of the evolution of services on the branch.

	Local trains		Boat trains	
	Weekdays	Sundays	Weekdays	Sundays
1870	5	3	-	-
1901	6	6	3	1
1930	12	5	6	3
1960	26	6	4	4
2000	20	14	4	3

To transport workers between Harwich and Parkeston Quay, a shuttle service was operated. It was available for public use and by 1930 there were 19 trips on weekdays and 11 on Sundays. By September 1956, there were 8 on weekdays and 7 on Sundays. By 1985, there were just two, on Sundays only.

Timetables for most years from 1882 to the 21st century have shown one or two trains daily between Ipswich and Parkeston Quay or its successor. The train linked the ships with the Midlands.

Hadleigh Branch

The initial service comprised five weekday and three Sunday trains, but the latter were soon withdrawn. There were some through coaches to London. These were slipped on their return.

In 1848, there were two trips to Bentley and two direct to Ipswich each weekday. 1849 brought a reduction to three trains, all to Bentley and in 1851 the figure was increased to four. Five was the number in 1852, with one reversing at Bentley on Tuesdays to serve Ipswich on its market day.

By 1853, the number was up to six and there were no through trains. A cut to three followed in 1855, but it was back to five in the next year. With the GER takeover in 1862, the frequency remained at four for a long period and a slip coach was restored for six months in 1876-77.

By 1889, there were five trains, with some working to Manningtree. Four was the usual number by 1913, with one through to Ipswich on Tuesdays. By 1920, it was the best ever, seven. Bus competition brought a reduction to five in 1924, this lasting until withdrawal in 1932.

LONDON, CHELMSFORD, COLCHESTER, HARWICH, IPSWICH, WOODBRIDGE, LOWESTOFT, YARMOUTH, & NORWICH.—G.E.

Miles.	For Fares, see pages 84 and 85.	1,2,3	1,2,3	1,2,3	1,2,3	1,2,3	1&2	1,2,3	1&2	1&2	1,2,3	1,2,3	1,2,3	1,2,3
		mrn	mrn	mrn	mrn	gov	mail	mrn	mrn	mrn	aft	aft	aft	aft
—	Bishopsgate ..dep	....	....	8 45	....	7 20	9 15	10 3	1110	1145	1215	1 0	2 30	3 5
1	Mile End	....	....	....	....	7 24	....	10 6	Wd	....	1218	1 3	....	3 8
3¼	Stratford	....	....	8 54	....	7 35	9 25	1015	1120	...	1227	1 12	2 39	3 17
4¾	Forest Gate	....	....	8 58	....	7 40	....	1019	1124	....	1231	1 16	2 43	3 21
7	Ilford, for Barking	....	....	9 4	....	7 48	....	1025	1130	....	1237	1 22	2 49	3 27
9½	Chadwell Heath	....	....	9 10	....	7 56	....	1031	....	....	1243	1 28	2 57	3 33
12	Romford 1	....	....	9 17	....	8 5	....	1038	1141	....	1250	1 35	3 2	3 40
14¾	Harold Wood	....	....	a	....	....	....	a	....	....	a	....	a	....
17¾	Brentwood	....	....	9 30	....	8 25	9 50	1052	12 0	....	1 3	1 52	3 15	3 52
23¼	Ingatestone	....	....	Stop	....	8 40	10 1	....	1213	....	Stop	2 5		Stop
29¼	Chelmsford	....	....		....	8 57	1015	....	1225	1236	....	2 17		....
38¼	Witham Junction 86	....	....	....	....	9 22	1032	....		1255	....	Stop	Saturdays only.	....
41¾	Kelvedon	....	....	....	....	9 34	1040	....	....	1 4	....	....		....
46¼	Marks Tey Junc. 86	....	1,2,3	....	....	9 50	....	....	....	1 16	....	....		....
51¾	Colchester ... arr	....	mrn	....	....	10 4	1057	....	....	1 26	....	....		....
	Tendring Hundred. All 1,2,3 class.													
—	Colchester dep	....	7 0	....	....		11 7	....	....	2 15	....	....		....
52	St. Botolph's	....	....	....	....	....	1119	....	....	2 27	....	....		....
53	Hythe	....	7 15	....	....	....	1123	....	....	2 31	....	....		....
55¾	Wivenhoe	....	7 25	....	....	....	1131	....	....	2 39	....	....		....
61	Brightlingsea	arr.	7 45	....	....	....	1150	....	....	3 10	....	....	....	....
57¼	Alresford	....	Stop	....	....	....	a	....	....	a	....		....	....
59	Thorington	....	....	....	....	....	a	....	....	a	....		....	....
60¼	Bentley Green	....	....	....	....	....	1146	....	....	2 54	....		....	....
62¼	Weeley	....	....	....	....	....	1152	....	....	2 59	....		....	....
64¼	Thorpe	....	....	....	....	....	1158	....	....	a	....		....	....
67	Kirby Cross	....	....	....	....	....	12 7	....	....	a	....		....	....
69½	Wltn-on-Naze	....	....	....	....	....	1215	....	....	3 20	....		....	....
—	Colchester ....dep	....	....	....	....	1012	11 0	....	....	1 20	....		....	....
55½	Ardleigh	....	....	....	....	1026	....	....	....	a	....		....	....
59	Manningtree	....	....	....	....	1038	1117	....	....	1 48	....		....	....
	Harwich Branch.													
—	Manningtree d	....	....	....	9 10		1125	....	....	1 55	....		....	....
60¾	Mistley	....	....	....	9 15		1130	....	....	2 0	....	Thursdays and Saturdays only.	....	....
62	Bradfield	....	....	....	a		a	....	....	a	....		....	....
67½	Wrabness	....	....	....	a		a	....	....	a	....		....	....
69½	Dovercourt	....	....	....	9 57		1157	....	....	2 27	....		....	....
69¾	Harwich ..arr	....	1,2,3	....	10 0		12 0	....	....	2 30	....		....	....
62½	Bentley Junction	....	mrn	....	Stop	1050	....	....	....	1 56	....		....	....
—	Bentley dp	....	9 0	....		1055	....	....	....	2 0	....		....	....
69¾	Hadleigh arr	....	9 25	1,2,3	....	1120	....	....	....	2 25	....		....	....
68	Ipswich ....arr	....	Stop	mrn	...	1110	1137	....	....	2 13	....		....	....
	Suffolk.													
—	Ipswich....dep	....		7 10	....		1150	....		2 23	....		....	....
71½	Westerfield	....	....	7 20	....		12 0	....		....	....		....	....
75¼	Bealings	....	....	7 29	....	....	12 9	....		2 39	....		....	....
78¼	Woodbridge		....	7 38	....	....	1218	....		2 47	....		....	....
79¼	Melton		....	7 43	....	....	1223	....	Thurs. only.	2 51	....	1,2,3	....	....
83¾	Wickham Mkt J		....	7 54	....	....	1233	....		3 1	....	aft	....	....
—	Wickhm Mkt J	All 1,2,3 cl.	....	8 0	....	....	1240	....		3 6	....	5 20	....	....
85½	Marlesford		....	8 8	....	....	1247	....		3 12	....	5 28	....	....
88	Parham		....	8 16	....	....	1257	....		3 22	....	5 37	....	....
90½	Framlinghm		....	8 25	....	....	1 5	....		3 30	....	5 45	....	....

Miles.	Station	1&2	1&2	1,2,3	1,2,3	1,2,3	1,2,3	1&2	1,2,3	1,2,3	Sundays (All 1,2,3 class)					
		c	exp	aft	aft	aft	aft	mail	aft	nigt	gov	mrn	aft	aft	mail	aft
—	Bishopsgate ..dep	3 35	4 25	4 35	5 30	6 30	7 30	8 30	10 0	1215	7 15	1020	2 45	4 30	8 30	1030
1	Mile End	....	....	....	....	....	....	....	....	....	7 19	1023	2 49	4 34	....	1033
3¼	Stratford	....	....	....	5 40	6 39	7 39	8 40	10 9	1224	7 29	1033	2 59	4 44	8 40	1043
4¾	Forest Gate	....	....	4 48	5 44	6 43	7 43	8 45	1013	1228	7 34	1039	3 4	4 49	....	1047
7	Ilford, for Barking	....	....	4 53	5 50	6 49	7 49	8 52	1019	1234	7 42	1045	3 10	4 55	8 49	1054
9½	Chadwell Heath	....	....	4 59	....	6 55	7 55	....	1025	....	7 49	1052	3 17	5 2	....	11 1
12	Romford 1	....	....	5 5	6 1	7 2	8 2	9 5	1032	1245	7 57	11 0	3 25	5 9	9 5	11 8
14¾	Harold Wood	....	....	a	....	a	a	....	....	....	....	a	....	a	....	....
17¾	Brentwood	4 12	....	5 22	6 16	7 20	8 15	9 22	1045	1257	8 15	1120	3 43	5 29	9 22	1125
23¼	Ingatestone	4 25	....	5 34	6 29	7 33		9 35		....	8 29	1134	3 56	5 42	9 35	
29¼	Chelmsford	4 39	5 13	5 46	6 43	7 45	....	9 48	...	....	8 46	1150	4 9	5 56	9 48	....
38¼	Witham Junction 86	4 58	5 30	6 0	7 2		....	10 3	....	....	9 11		4 28		10 3	....
41¾	Kelvedon	5 7	....	....	7 10	....	....	1018	....	....	9 22	....	4 38		1018	....
46¼	Marks Tey Junc. 86	5 19	5 45	....	7 20	....	....	a	....	....	9 37	....	4 50		1027	....
51¾	Colchester ... arr	5 29	5 55	....	7 30	....	....	1038	....	....	9 50	....	5 3		1038	....
	Tendring Hundred. All 1,2,3 class.															
—	Colchester dep	6 5		....	Stop	....	....	....	....	....	....	....	....		....	....
52	St. Botolph's	6 17		....	....	....	....	....	....	....	....	....	....		....	....
53	Hythe	6 21		....	....	....	....	....	....	....	....	....	....		....	....
55¾	Wivenhoe	6 29		....	....	....	....	....	....	....	....	....	....		....	....
61	Brightlingsea	6 50		....	....	....	....	....	....	....	....	....	....		....	....
57¼	Alresford	a		....	....	....	....	....	....	....	....	....	....		....	....
59	Thorington	a		....	....	....	....	....	....	....	....	....	....		....	....
60¼	Bentley Green	6 44		....	....	....	....	....	....	....	....	....	....		....	....
62¼	Weeley	6 49		....	....	....	....	....	....	....	....	....	....		....	....
64¼	Thorpe	6 54		....	....	....	....	....	....	....	....	....	....		....	....
67	Kirby Cross	7 3		....	....	....	....	....	....	....	....	....	....		....	....
69½	Wltn-on-Naze	7 10		....	....	....	....	....	....	....	....	....	....		....	....
—	Colchester ....dep	5 32	5 58	....	....	....	....	1042	....	....	9 57	....	5 8		1042	....
55½	Ardleigh	5 42	....	....	....	....	....	a	....	....	10 9	....	5 18		a	....
59	Manningtree	5 52	6 15	....	....	....	....	11 0	....	....	1020	....	5 28		11 0	....
	Harwich Branch.															
—	Manningtree d	6 26		....	....	....	....	11 5	....	....	[illegible]	....	5 35		11 5	....
60¾	Mistley	6 31		....	....	....	....	1110	....	....	[illegible]	....	5 40		1110	....
62	Bradfield	a		....	....	....	....	....	....	....	a	....	a		....	....
67½	Wrabness	a		....	....	....	....	....	....	....	a	....	a		....	....
69½	Dovercourt	6 57		....	....	....	....	1135	....	....	1057	....	6 7		1135	...
69¾	Harwich ..arr	7 0		....	....	....	....	1140	....	....	11 0	....	6 10		1140	...
62½	Bentley Junction	6 1	....	....	....	....	....	a	....	....	1032	....	5 38		a	...
—	Bentley dp	6 17	....	....	....	....	....	....	....	....	....	....	....		....	....
69¾	Hadleigh arr	6 42	....	....	....	....	....	....	....	....	....	....	....		....	....
68	Ipswich ....arr	6 18	6 35	....	....	....	....	1125	....	....	1050	....	5 55		1125	....
	Suffolk.															
—	Ipswich....dep	6 45		....	....	....	....	....	....	....	....	....	6 5		....	....
71½	Westerfield	6 55		....	....	....	....	....	....	....	....	....	6 15		....	....
75¼	Bealings	7 4		....	....	....	....	....	....	....	....	....	6 24		....	....
78¼	Woodbridge	7 12		....	....	....	....	....	....	....	....	....	6 32		....	....
79¼	Melton	7 16		....	....	....	....	....	....	....	....	....	6 36		....	....
83¾	Wickham Mkt J	7 26		....	....	....	....	....	....	....	....	....	6 46		....	....
—	Wickhm Mkt J	7 58		....	....	....	....	....	....	....	....	....	....		....	....
85½	Marlesford	8 6		....	....	....	....	....	....	....	....	....	....		....	....
88	Parham	8 15		....	....	....	....	....	....	....	....	....	....		....	....
90½	Framlinghm	8 23		....	....	....	....	....	....	....	....	....	....		....	....

RETURN TICKETS at Single Fares are issued every Sunday by all Trains to and from all Stations on the Eastern Union Line, available for the day only.

December 1870

MANNINGTREE and HARWICH.—Great Eastern.

Miles from Manningtree.	Fares from London. Single. 1 cl. s. d.	Single. 3 cl. s. d.	Return. 1 cl. s. d.	Return. 3 cl. s. d.	Down.	Week Days. mrn	mrn	mrn	aft	aft	aft	aft	aft	aft	aft	aft	Sundays. mrn	aft	aft	aft	mrn	aft	aft
	....	....	....	....	Liverpool Street, London 236 ....dep.	....	8 55	1145	2 25	5 30	....	7 15	....	8 30	8 40	8 40	9 0	....	4 15	....	....	8 30	8 30
					York 277 .... "	....	....	....	....	1025	1252	....	3 50	Continental Express.	Continental Express.	3 50	....	....	....	....	1150	Continental Express.	....
					Doncaster 277 ...... "	....	....	8 10	....	1116	1 42	....	4 38			4 38	....	....	....	....	2 35		....
					Ipswich 240 .... "	8 7	1016	1 29	3b35	6a2	8 0	....	....			9 30	9 40	3 5	....	6 25	7 45		8 35
	....	....	....	....	Manningtree ....dep.	8 40	11 0	1 58	4 30	7 15	....	9 5	....			1015	1044	3 30	5 50	6 52	8 5		10 3
1¼	11 8	5 2	17 6	10 4	Mistley	8 46	11 6	2 4	4 36	7 21	8 19	....	....			1021	1050	3 36	5 56	6 58	8 11		10 9
3	1110	5 3½	17 9	10 7	Bradfield	8 49	11 9	2 7	4 39	7 24	....	....	....			1024	1053	3 39	5 59	7 1	....		1012
5½	12 2	5 6	18 3	11 0	Wrabness	8 56	1116	2 14	4 46	7 31	....	....	....			1031	11 0	3 46	6 6	7 8	....		1019
9½	1210	5 10	19 6	11 8	Harwich { Parkeston Quay	9 6	1126	2 24	4 56	7 42	8 37	9 23	9 27	9 57	10 7	1039	11 8	3 55	6 14	7 16	8 27	9 57	1029
10¾	13 0	5 11	19 8	1110	Harwich { Dovercourt	9 11	1131	2 29	5 1	7 47	8 42	9 28	9 37	....	1019	1046	1113	4 0	6 19	7 21	8 32	10 9	1034
11¼	13 3	511½	20 0	1111	Harwich { Town ....arr.	9 14	1134	2 32	5 4	7 50	8 45	9 31	9 40	....	1022	1049	1116	4 3	6 22	7 24	8 35	1012	1037

Mls	Fares. Single. 1 cl.	Single. 3 cl.	Return. 1 cl.	Return. 3 cl.	Up.	Week Days. mrn	mrn	mrn	mrn	aft	aft	aft (Except Saturdays.)	aft (Sats. only.)	aft	aft	Sundays. mrn	mrn	mrn	aft	aft	aft	
—					Harwich { Town ....dep.	6e35	7 45	9e25	9 50	1245	3 10	5 45	5 55	8 15	9 10	6 50	8 40	9 0	5 0	6 7	9 15	....
½					Harwich { Dovercourt	6 38	7 48	9 28	9 53	1248	3 13	5 48	5 58	8 18	9 13	6 53	8 43	9 3	5 3	6 10	9 18	....
2	0 3	0 1	0 4	0 2	Harwich { Parkeston Quay	7 0	7 55	9 39	9 57	1252	3 17	5 52	6 2	8 21	9 16	7 0	8 50	9 10	5 7	6 14	9 24	....
5¾	1 0	0 5½	1 7	0 11	Wrabness	....	8 5	....	10 7	1 2	3 27	6 2	6 12	8 31	9 25	....	....	9 19	5 15	6 24	9 33	....
8¼	1 5	0 8½	2 3	1 5	Bradfield	....	8 11	....	1013	1 8	3 33	6 8	6 18	....	9 31	....	....	9 25	5 21	6 30	9 39	....
9¾	1 8	0 9½	2 6	1 7	Mistley	....	8 15	9 52	1017	1 12	3 37	6 12	6 22	8 40	9 35	....	....	9 29	5 25	6 34	9 44	....
11½	2 1	011½	3 1	1 11	Manningtree 236, 240 ..arr.	....	8 20	....	1022	1 17	3 42	6 17	6 27	8 45	9 40	....	....	9 35	5 30	6 39	9 50	....
20	3 0	1 8½	5 0	3 0	Ipswich 236 ....arr.	7 30	9 50	1010	1112	1 48	4 40	7 30	7 30	9 15	1025	7 33	9 20	1048	5 54	....	1018	....
—	22 8	150½	45 4	30 1	Doncaster 276 ...... "	1159	3 28	3 28	6c34	9 0	....	....	....	....	....	....	2 35	....	....	....	....	....
—	27 2	178½	54 4	[illegible]	York 276 .... "	1256	4 21	4 21	....	9 52	....	....	....	....	....	....	4 35	....	....	....	....	....
70½	13 3	511½	20 0	1111	240 London (Liverpool St.) "	....	1026	....	1226	3 30	5 50	8 5	8 15	....	....	....	....	1130	....	8 52	....	....

a Leaves at 6 12 aft. on Saturdays. **b** Leaves at 4 5 aft. on Tuesdays. **c** *Via* Sudbury. **e** Through Carriages to York.

January 1901

HARWICH and PARKESTON.– G.E.

Harwich (Town Station) **to Parkeston** at 4¾ (Mondays only), 5 (except Mondays), 5¾, 6 20, 6 35, 7½, 7 45, 8½, 9 25, 9½, 9 50, 10½, and 11½ mrn.; 12 30, 12 45, 1¾, 2½, 3 10, 3½, 4½, 5¼, 5¾ (except Saturdays), 5 55, 6 (Saturdays only), 6 45, 7½, 8 15, 9 10, 9 30, and 10¾ aft. SUNDAYS at 5, 5¾, 6½, 6 50, 7½, 8½, 8 40, 9, 9½, and 10½ mrn.; 12¾, 2½, 5, 6 7, 7½, 8½, 9¼, and 10 aft.

Parkeston to Harwich (Town Station) at 4½, 5½, 6, 7, 8, 9, 9 6, 10, 11, and 11 26 mrn.; 12 noon; 1, 2, 2 24, 3, 4, 4¾, 4 56, 5 35, 6¼, 7, 7 42, 7 50, 8 37, 9 23, 9 27, 10 7, and 10 39 aft. SUNDAYS at 4½, 5½, 6, 7, 8, 9, 10, 10¾, and 11 8 mrn.; 1¼, 2½, 3 55, 6 14, 7 16, 8, 8 27, 9, 9 57, 10 39, and 10 40 aft.

☞ All Trains call at Dovercourt.

Table 28— *continued*

HARWICH and FELIXSTOWE MOTOR BOAT SERVICES

(Weather and other circumstances permitting)

	Week Days	Sundays
Harwich Pier to Felixstowe (Dock) ..	8 0, 9 55 and 11 55 am 2 10, 2 55 and 5 25 pm	10 55 am 2†15, 3 30 and 4†50 pm
Felixstowe (Dock) to Harwich Pier ..	8 25 and 10 30 am 12 30, 2 35, 3 30 and 5 45 pm	11 30 am 3 0, 4 0 and 5 30 pm

† Via Shotley

Table 29— *continued*

HARWICH TOWN, DOVERCOURT BAY, HARWICH (Parkeston Quay) and MANNINGTREE

Week Days

Miles		am	am		am	am		am P R	am	am M R	am		am T		am	am		pm	pm	pm Y	pm	pm R
	Harwich Town .. dep	5 15	5 56	..	6 41	7 18	..	..	7 29	..	8 20	..	8 46	..	9 58	1120	..	12 5	1220	1245	1 20	..
½	Dovercourt Bay	5 18	5 59		6 45	7 21			7 32		8 23		8 50		10 2	1124		12 8	1224	1249	1 23	
1¾	**Harwich** Parkeston Qy arr	5 22	6 2	..	6 48	7 24	..	..	7 36	..	8 27	..	8 55	..	10 5	1127	..	1212	1227	1254	1 27	..
	Harwich Parkeston Qy dep		6 4		6 50	7 26		7 42		8 0			8 56		10 7	1129			1229	1255		D1N30
2¼	**Harwich** Parkeston Qy West	..	..	..	..	..	..		..	..	..	..	..	..	..	..	..	..	..	..	..	
5¾	Wrabness		6 12		6 58	7 34		The Hook Continental					9 8		10 15	1137			1237			The Scandinavian
8¼	Bradfield	..	6 19	..	7 5	7 41	..		..	..	..	..	..	..	10 22	1144	..	..	1244	..	..	
9½	Mistley		6 23		7 9	7 45							9 17		10 26	1148			1248	1 11		
11¼	**Manningtree** .. .. arr	..	6 28	..	7 14	7 50	..		..	..	..	..	9 22	..	10 31	1153	..	..	1253	..	..	
20½	5 Ipswich .... arr				7 54	8 23				8 30			9 45		11 21	1219			1S23	1 33		
19	5 Colchester .. .. „	..	6 49	..	7 35	8L26	..		..	..	..	..	9 40	..	10 52	1219	..	..	1 26	..	..	
70¾	5 **London** (L'pool St) „		8 24		9 1	9 43		9 14					1116		12A40	1H45			3J 0			3N 7

Week Days—*continued*

	pm C	pm C	pm	pm	pm C		pm	pm	pm	pm R		pm		pm R	pm	pm		pm	pm	pm	
	Except Saturdays	Saturdays only			Except Saturdays					Runs 3rd Oct. to 21st April incl. The Day Continental				Runs until 1st October and from 23rd April The Day Continental							
Harwich Town .. dep	1 35	1 38	1 50	3 25	4 18	..	4 53	5 21	5 50	..	..	6 30		..	7 32	8 20	..	9 30	9 45	1019	..
Dovercourt Bay	1 39	1 42	1 53	3 28	4 21		4 57	5 25	5 53			6 34			7 36	8 23		9 34	9 48	1022	
Harwich Parkeston Qy arr	1 42	1 45	1 57	3 31	4 26	..	5 0	5 28	5 57	..	..	6 37		..	7 39	8 27	..	9 37	9 52	1026	..
Harwich Parkeston Qy dep	1 45	1 48		3 33	4 28		5 2	5 30		6 20		6 39		7 25	7 41			9 39			
Harwich Parkeston Qy West	..	..	..	..	..	..	..	..	..	6 30	..	..		7 35	..	..	..	..	..	..	..
Wrabness	1 53	1 56		3 41	4 36		5 10	5 38				6 47			7 49			9 47			
Bradfield	2 0	2 3	..	3 48	4 43	..	5 17	5 45	..		..	6 54			7 56	..	..	..	..	..	..
Mistley	2 4	2 7		3 51	4 47		5 21	5 49				6 58			8 0			9 54			
Manningtree .. .. arr	2 9	2 12	..	3 57	4 52	..	5 26	5 54	..		..	7 3			8 5	..	..	9 59	..	..	..
5 Ipswich .... arr		3 5		4d28			5 51	6 12				7 38			8 53			1025			
5 Colchester .. .. „	2 23	2 26	..	4 26	5 7	..	5 56	6 24	..		..	7 20			8 31	..	..	1027	..	..	..
5 **London** (L'pool St) „	4 13	4 8		5 5	6 39			7 45		8G 6		9 2		9 6	9 56			12 5			

Sundays

	am	am	am P R		am	am C	am	am		pm C	pm R	pm	pm	pm	pm R	pm	pm R	pm	pm	pm	
			The Hook Continental								The Scandinavian				Runs 2nd Oct. to 15th April incl. The Day Continental		Runs on 25th September and from 22nd April The Day Continental				
Harwich Town .. dep	5 15	5 45	..	..	7 43	8 55	9 55	1127	..	1235	..	1 20	1 46	5 5	..	6 28	..	7 42	9 45	1019	..
Dovercourt Bay	5 18	5 48			7 46	8 59	9 58	1131		1239		1 23	1 49	5 8		6 31		7 46	9 48	1022	
Harwich Parkeston Qy arr	5 22	5 52	..	..	7 50	9 2	10 1	1134	..	1242	..	1 27	1 53	5 11	..	6 34	..	7 49	9 52	1026	..
Harwich Parkeston Qy dep			7 42			9 4	10 2	1136		1246	K1015			5 13	6 20	6 36	7 35	7 51			
Harwich Parkeston Qy West	..	..		..	..	..	..	..	..	..		..	..	..	6 30	..	7 45	..	..	..	..
Wrabness						9 12		1144		1254				5 21		6 44		7 59			
Bradfield	..	..		..	..	9 19	..	1151	..	1 1		..	..	5 28		6 51		8 6	..	..	..
Mistley						9 23	1014	1155		1 5				5 32		6 55		8 10			
Manningtree .. .. arr	..	..		..	..	9 28	1019	12 0	..	1 10		..	..	5 37		7 0		8 15	..	..	..
5 Ipswich .... arr							11B5	1230						6 29				8 38			
5 Colchester .. .. „	..	..		..	..	9 46	1054	1221	..	1 28		..	..	6 1		7 41		8 49	..	..	..
5 **London** (L'pool St) „			9 14			1137	1240	2 11		4 53	2 50			7 35	8 0	9 9	9 20	1018			

A On Saturdays arrives Liverpool Street 12 35 pm
B On 25th September and from 22nd April, arrives Ipswich 10 52 am
C Through Train Harwich Town to Colchester
D This train may depart *earlier* than shown if the steamer from Esbjerg has arrived. Intending local passengers are advised to confirm the departure time at Harwich (Parkeston Quay) station on the day of travel
d On Saturdays arrives Ipswich 4 19 pm
E or E Except Saturdays
G On Saturdays arrives Liverpool Street 8 0 pm
H On Saturdays arrives Liverpool Street 1 40 pm
J On Saturdays arrives Liverpool Street 3 21 pm
K 25th December excepted
L On Saturdays arrives Colchester 8 21 am
M Through Train to Liverpool (Central) arr 3 27 pm (Tables 5, 35, 40, 62 and 68)
N Runs on Tuesdays, Thursdays and Fridays until 13th October; Saturday 15th October; Tuesday 18th October; Thursdays only 20th October to 19th April (except 22nd December); Wednesday 21st December; Wednesdays and Fridays commencing 25th April
P Conveys only passengers holding tickets from the Continent
R Refreshment Car
S or S Saturdays only
T Through Train Harwich Town to Liverpool Street
Y Through Train to Peterborough (North) arr 4 45 pm (Tables 35 & 40)

7 May 1956

16 May 1983

Harwich to Manningtree and Ipswich — Mondays to Saturdays

Miles					SO	SX		A The Hook Continental		SX			SX		B SO		A E
0	**Harwich Town** .. d	..	..	06 48	06 48	..	..	..	07 53	..	08 32	09 04	..	10 30	11 04	..
¾	Dovercourt .. d			06 50	06 50				07 55		08 34	09 06		10 33	11 06	
1¾	Harwich Parkeston Quay .. a	..	..	06 53	06 53	..	..	..	07 58	..	08 37	09 09	..	10 35	11 09	..
	d			06 54	06 54	07 17	07 50		07 59		08 38	09 10		10 36	11 10	12 10
5¾	**Wrabness** .. d	..	..	07 01	07 01	..		..	08 06	..	08 45	09 17	..		11 17	
9½	**Mistley** .. d			07 07	07 07				08 12		08 51	09 23			11 23	
11¼	**Manningtree** .. a	..	..	07 11	07 11	..		..	08 16	..	08 55	09 27	..		11 27	
20¼	11 **Ipswich** .. a			07 29	07 29	07 47			08 42		09b50	09 50			11 48	
66¾	11 **Norwich** .. a	..	..	..	..	09 41		..	09 41	..	10b47	10 47	..		12 45	
19¼	11 **Colchester** .. a			07 26	07 40				08 34		09 13	09 49		11 03	11 49	
70¼	11 **London Liverpool Street** ⊖ .. a	..	..	08 33	08 38	..	09 14	..	09 35	..	10 12	10 44	..	12 14	12 44	13 28

		C	A G			D SX		SO		A E The Day Continental		A G The Day Continental		SO	SX	
Harwich Town .. d	12 07	..	..	13 04	15 04	16 20	..	16 20	17 04	..	..	..	18 35	19 11	19 17	20 35
Dovercourt .. d	12 09			13 06	15 06	16 22		16 22	17 06				18 37	19 13	19 19	20 37
Harwich Parkeston Quay .. a	12 12	..	..	13 09	15 09	16 25	..	16 25	17 09	..	..	..	18 40	19 16	19 22	20 40
d		12 20	12 46	13 10	15 10	16 26		16 26	17 10	18 00	18 07	18 55	18 41	19 17	19 23	20 41
Wrabness .. d	..	12 28		13 17	15 17	16 33	..	16 33	17 17		..		18 48	19 24	19 30	20 48
Mistley .. d		12 34		13 23	15 23	16 39		16 39	17 23				18 54	19 30	19 36	20 54
Manningtree .. a	..	..		13 27	15 27	16 43	..	16 43	17 27		..		18 58	19 34	19 40	20 58
11 **Ipswich** .. a		12 53		13 48	15 48	17 01		17 01	17f51		18 37		19k32	19 52	20 01	21e48
11 **Norwich** .. a	..	14n05		14 45	16 45	18 18	..	..	18f51		19p35		20k31	20 49	21 01	22c48
11 **Colchester** .. a				13 49	15 49				17 49				19 12		19 57	21 12
11 **London Liverpool Street** ⊖ .. a	..	..	14 11	14 44	16 45	..	..	..	18 45	19 23	..	20 18	20 27	..	21g04	22h29

A Limited accommodation— Passengers not holding tickets to/from the Continent may be directed to other trains
B 28 May to 10 September
C To Peterborough arr. 14 55 (Table 18)
D To Stowmarket arr 17 20 (Table 11)
E Until 24 September and from 24 October
G 26 September to 22 October
H 29 May to 18 September
J Until 18 September and from 23 October
K 25 September to 16 October
b Saturdays arr. Ipswich 09 52, Norwich 10 49
c Saturdays arr. 22 52
e Saturdays arr. 21 54
f Saturdays arr. Ipswich 17 48, Norwich 18 46
g Change at Colchester
h Saturdays arr. 22 27
j Saturdays arr. 20 18
k Mondays to Fridays
n Saturdays 18 June to 17 September
p Saturdays arr. 19 32

1. Harwich Branch
MANNINGTREE

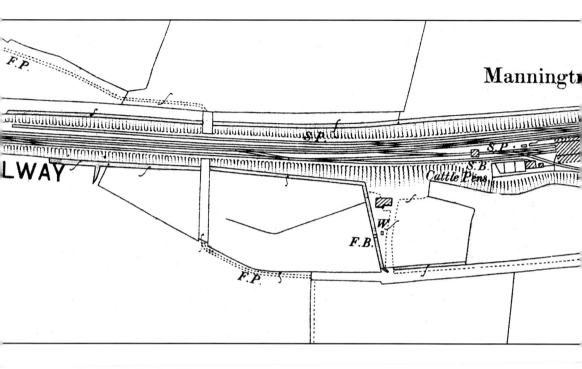

1.   The back of East Junction Box comes into view as we move up the lane from Manningtree. The box was at the southern apex of the triangular junction and the down signals are on the left. We are looking west. (P.Laming coll.)

II.   The 1897 edition has the goods yard to the left of the main building and South Junction signal box (S.B.) inside the junction. It was moved north of the main line in 1926 and was known as South Junction Box.

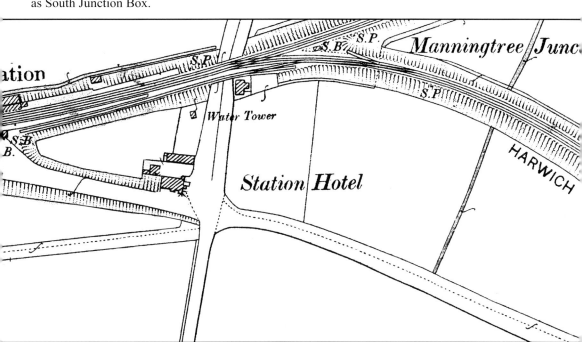

2.   After a walk of about one mile from the village, we are just to the south of the Station Hotel. On the right is the inclined station approach and the long up platform canopy. Close to us is a flooded field. (P.Laming coll.)

3.	We are near the bridge seen in picture 1 and are looking north at East Junction Box and the flat land of Essex. The box had 15 levers and was in use from 1882 until 1926. (R.R.Clow coll.)

4.	North Junction Box was nearest the River Stour Viaduct. Immediately beyond it is Cattawade Viaduct. The box was in use from 1882 until 7th June 1925. (R.R.Clow coll.)

5.	Running to London is "Britannia" class 4-6-2 no. 70035 *Rudyard Kipling*. The date is unknown, but we have a rare view of the down siding. Its platform was not used by passengers. (Dr. J. Westall/A. Vaughan coll.)

6.	An eastward panorama from 7th January 1980 clearly shows signalling in transition, but unclear is the level crossing. It is close to the resited South Junction Box, which closed on 27th September 1984. There is a supplementary underpass of limited headroom. (D.C.Pearce)

7.   No. 37051 approaches the station with a boat train from Harwich on the same day. It is the goods shed and yard which were available to lease. (D.C.Pearce)

8.   The down side canopy had been removed and the up one shortened, not long before this photograph was taken on 25th August 1983. (R.F.Roberts/SLS coll.)

9.   The GER buildings were all still intact when recorded on 10th September 1988 and the wires were in place. (F.Hornby)

10.   The level crossing is evident and on the right is the line to the bay, which was used by most trains from Harwich. Anglia Railways no. 86221 *B.B.C Look East* departs for Norwich on 4th February 2001. (D.A.Pollock)

11.   The station had its busiest ever period when Ipswich tunnel was closed for alteration to allow larger containers to pass through it. A bus service was provided from 19th July to 5th September 2004 and this is the result in a field on the north side of the station. (B.I.Nathan)

Other views of this area can be seen in the *Shenfield to Ipswich* album.

MISTLEY

12.   Track repairs behind a passenger train was an unusual subject for a postcard. In the background are some of the maltings, which were developed in the second half of the 19th century. In the first half, there were 16 public houses in Mistley. (P.Laming coll.)

13.   Four horses, one goat, one dog and 18 two-legged creatures add interest to another unusual postcard view of the station. Horses were often used for shunting, as well as carting goods. (R.R.Clow coll.)

III.　　The 1897 survey features the long curved incline to the docks, which was in use until about 1900, haulage being mainly equine. A more direct, but steeper, route followed with reversal points part way. The dock had been extended in 1849. The first signal box was in use from the doubling in 1882 until 1898 and it had 27 levers. The second had 30 and lasted until 1985.

Jetty

Malthouse

DOCK

E R

Inn

Fn

Smithy

Malthouse

W

S T O

Union Bdy

C. C. at L.W.

DOCK

Quay

M.P.

Water Works

Malthouse

Malthouses

Station

Goods Shed

L.B.

S.P.

S.B.

S.P.

S.P.

The Elms

o W

School

W

P

Malthouses

BECKFORD ROAD

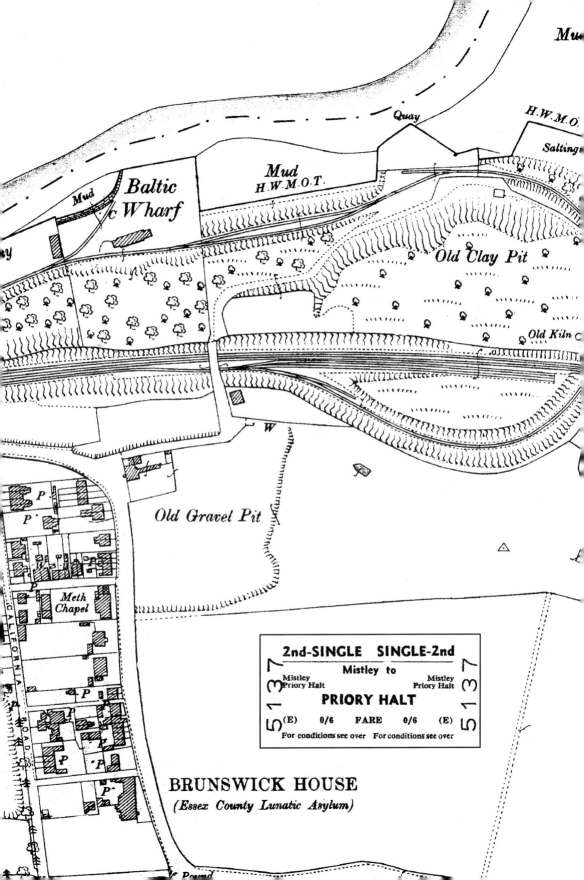

Mu

H.W.M.O.

Saltings

Quay

Mud
H.W.M.O.T.

**Baltic
Wharf**

Mud

Old Clay Pit

Old Kiln

W

Old Gravel Pit

*Meth
Chapel*

P

P

P

P

P

P

P

P

CALIFORNIA ROAD

BRUNSWICK HOUSE
(Essex County Lunatic Asylum)

Pound

14. An uncluttered view of the down platform in the 1930s includes particularly tall chimneys and pots to give a good draught in this windy location. The tall signal has a co-acting arm. (G.Austin/R.R.Clow coll.)

15. Climbing the incline some time in 1950 is class J15 0-6-0 no. 65458. The reversal point is in the background. (R.R.Clow coll.)

16.   Seen on 15th March 1960 is another member of the same class and it is reaching the top of the incline, behind the malthouses. (Colour-Rail.com)

17.   No. 47106 is working an up mixed freight from Harwich on 19th May 1977. The dock line disappears into dense forest, which was cleared before the next photograph was taken. (B.Morrison)

18.   This is the view up the incline from the reversal points and features modern grain stores, along with historic maltings. Their opposite elevation is in the next picture and both are from 7th January 1980. (D.C.Pearce)

➔   19. Much of the malt output was destined for whisky, vinegar, confectionery and yeast breads. Three ships per week on average visited the docks in 2008. The first dock line was on the right and the final one is on the left in this photograph. (D.C.Pearce)

➔   20. Barley came from various parts of the world to the maltings and about 400 people were employed in them in 1900. Much of the malt then went by barge to breweries in and around London. (R.F.Roberts/SLS coll.)

21.   The 16.20 from Harwich Town to Ipswich is coming to a stand on 25th August 1983. Mistley High Street bridge was rebuilt, half at a time, in 1984. (R.F.Roberts/SLS coll.)

➔   22.   A westward view in 1984 has the overgrown dock line on the right and the down platform in the distance. The eastern half of the bridge has been removed and the lattice structure is temporary. (D.C.Pearce)

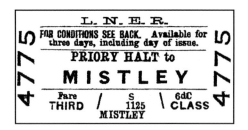

➔   23.   We extend our survey in 1984 by looking at the access to the goods yard, from a train. There was a 30cwt. crane in 1938, when there were three private sidings nearby. (D.C.Pearce)

24.   The goods yard had been rearranged by
1984 and grain wagons were to be seen in two of
the sidings. The maltings later expanded across
the area on the left carrying the sidings. The
maltings were still busy in 2011. (D.C.Pearce)

➔   25. The bridge had suffered from the
wrong type of motorist when the junction details
were photographed in 1984. The new abutments
are half finished. They would support a series of
pre-cast concrete beams. (D.C.Pearce)

➔   26. The entrance gives the impression of an early weather forecasting station, but devoid of
the two necessary characters. Mistley's population was 976 in 1841 and 2053 in 2010. The final
three views are from 29th March 1986. (J.M.Rickard/Colour-Rail.com)

27.	The rebuilt road bridge gave improved clearance for the high voltage wires and the platforms could accommodate four coaches. The up refuge siding was still usable in 2006, as was the down loop. (J.M.Rickard/Colour-Rail.com)

28.	The chimney declares EDME MALT EXTRACT WORKS, while the station retains most of its original features, albeit surrounded by electric lights and traction supplies. EDME stands for English Diastatic Malt Extract. (J.M.Rickard/Colour-Rail.com)

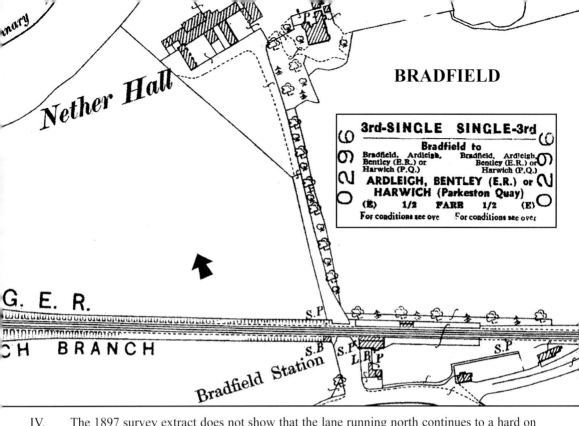

BRADFIELD

3rd-SINGLE		SINGLE-3rd	

0296 **Bradfield to** 0296

Bradfield, Ardleigh, Bentley (E.R.) or Harwich (P.Q.)   Bradfield, Ardleigh, Bentley (E.R.) or Harwich (P.Q.)

ARDLEIGH, BENTLEY (E.R.) or HARWICH (Parkeston Quay)

(E)   1/2   **FARE**   1/2   (E)

For conditions see over   For conditions see over

Nether Hall

G. E. R.

CH BRANCH   *Bradfield Station*

IV.   The 1897 survey extract does not show that the lane running north continues to a hard on the River Stour.

29.   The splendid architecture would complement the nearby Nether Hall with its numerous outbuildings. The local population was modest: 730 in 1901 and 811 in 1961. (P.Laming coll.)

30.   Two single gates were provided, hence the massive tall post, which carried hinged stay rods. The station closed on 2nd July 1956. There was a 12-lever signal box from 1882 until 1924. (P.Laming coll.)

31.   The lack of brickwork was made up for with a profusion of signs. Note that the old wicket gates had been retained for pedestrians. The user worked barriers came into use in October 1985. (J.M.Rickard/Colour-Rail.com)

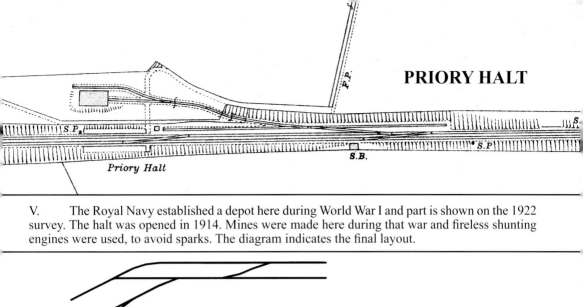

PRIORY HALT

Priory Halt

V.   The Royal Navy established a depot here during World War I and part is shown on the 1922 survey. The halt was opened in 1914. Mines were made here during that war and fireless shunting engines were used, to avoid sparks. The diagram indicates the final layout.

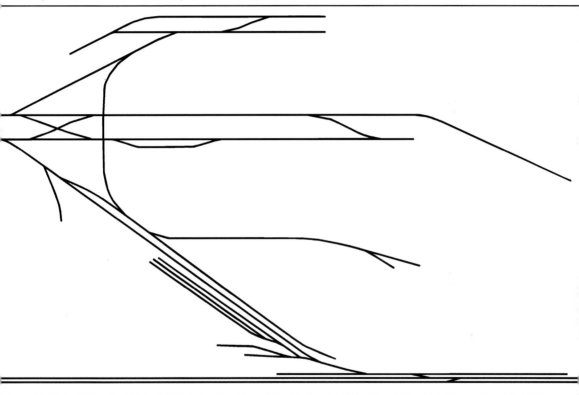

32.   An eastward view in 1957 reveals the simplicity of the facilities and includes the signal box, which is close to the points to the depot. The halt closed on 1st February 1965, having been "For Admiralty employees only" at various periods. The box was in use from 1918 until 26th October 1966, although the depot closed in 1964. It had 18 levers. (R.R.Clow coll.)

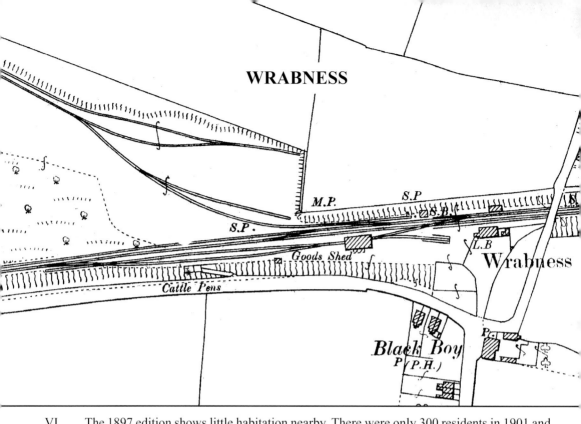

WRABNESS

VI.   The 1897 edition shows little habitation nearby. There were only 300 residents in 1901 and 379 in 1961. The sidings top left were extended to the riverside during World War II to accommodate a massive rail-mounted gun, which protected the river estuary. The Naval Sub-Depot at Copperas had a signal box named Primrose. It had a 16-lever frame and was open from 1st February 1919 until 16th April 1964, when the depot closed. This was two miles east of the station.

33.   We start our survey with a westward panorama from the road bridge in about 1900. The goods shed contained a 30cwt crane. (P.Laming coll.)

34.   The local unusual postcard producer was marketing this novel product in about 1916. The lower windows are for the machine room, where the interlocking equipment was kept out of view. (R.R.Clow coll.)

35.   The goods yard is seen in around 1930, along with a coach body, which was probably used for additional seasonal staff. Freight ceased to be handled after 7th December 1964. (R.R.Clow coll.)

36.   A serious problem arose on 29th
January 1929 during single line working.
Class B17 no. 2804 *Elveden* was derailed,
along with at least the leading van.
(R.R.Clow coll.)

➔   37.   The 08.56 Peterborough to Harwich
Parkeston Quay is seen on 12th October 1977, when
a waiting room and one for ladies was still on offer.
One crossover had been retained.
(T.Heavyside)

➔   38.   Three more views from the same day
enable us to enjoy passing trains, typical of that
era. No. 31107 is westbound with car carriers
from Harwich Town. (T.Heavyside)

39.   No. 37036 is hauling Mk.I coaches forming the 09.40 Liverpool Street to Harwich Parkeston Quay "Day Continental" service. No footbridge was provided, passengers crossing under the careful eye of the signalman. (T.Heavyside)

→   40. No. 47009 is departing with the 12.40pm Harwich Parkeston Quay to Peterborough. The numerous telephone wires were still uninsulated. (T.Heavyside)

→   41. A stopping train departs west on 1st January 1982, under a cloud of diesel smoke. A seat of some antiquity adorns the up platform, but it would soon vanish. (J.M.Rickard/Colour-Rail.com)

42.   This perfect   scene is only spoilt by thoughtless pole positioning. The date is 27th August 1983 and even the belfry remains in place. (J.M.Rickard/Colour-Rail.com)

➔   43. It is 1984 and masts have arrived, along with new track panels. Two crossovers were provided for use in emergencies. (D.C.Pearce)

➔   44. The nearest bridge offered adequate clearance for the imminent wire, but the one beyond it had been rebuilt. The signal box is seen in 1984, it closing on 29th September 1985. It had 25 levers and was moved bodily to Nunnery Junction on the Colne Valley Railway on 10th January 1988. (D.C.Pearce)

45.　　It is 29th March 1986 and the wires are up at this historic station, which had been well conserved during the modernisation process. (J.M.Rickard/Colour-Rail.com)

➜　46. Seen on the same day, the north elevation remained unspoilt. The platform edge had been raised long ago. (J.M.Rickard/Colour-Rail.com)

➜　47. Both platforms could accommodate four coaches and the up one is seen on 10th September 1988. By that time, sadly, slates were missing, windows had been broken and facilities were only signed for gentlemen. Demolition took place soon after, despite a preservation scheme having been finalised. (F.Hornby)

HARWICH PARKESTON QUAY WEST

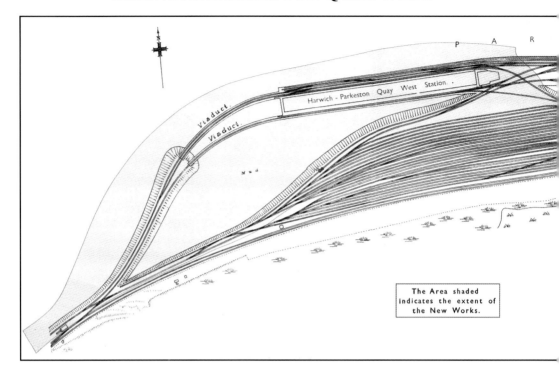

Harwich - Parkeston Quay West Station.

The Area shaded indicates the extent of the New Works.

48.   This area was open to passengers from 1st October 1934 until 1st May 1972 and the berths were on the far side. This design minimised the land reclamation required and is seen in June 1934. (R.R.Clow coll.)

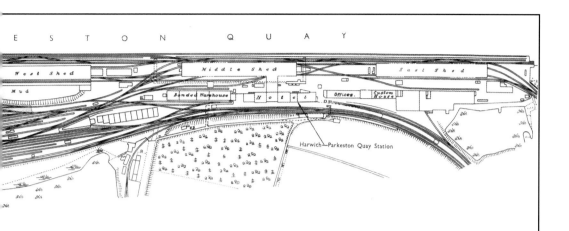

West Shed

Middle Shed

East Shed

Mud

Bonded Warehouse   H o t e l   Offices.   Custom House

Harwich—Parkeston Quay Station

VIIa.   As usual, we examine the stations in journey order, but readers who would prefer to understand the development of the port chronologically should see the pictures in the following order: 87-101, 53-75, 48-52 and then 76-79. This is the official plan from 1934 and has Parkeston Goods Junction signal box on the left.

49.   A closer view at the west end has the lines to the berths on the left and those on the right were used mostly by passenger trains. The cranes on this quay could lift five tons. (Dr.J.Westall/A.Vaughan coll.)

50.   LNER class B17/6 4-6-0 no. 2823 *Lambton Castle* heads the "Flushing Continental". The cantilevered roof design gave an uncluttered platform, but resulted in lengthy rainwater pipes. (NRM/R.R.Clow coll.)

→   51. This westward panorama is from 14th May 1956. For many years the "Day Hook" and Rotterdam ferries sailed from here, while the "Night Hook" and Danish vessels used the old Quay. (R.M.Casserley)

→   52. Seen on the same day is the "Day Continental" which left Liverpool Street at 9.30am for many years. LNER lighting was still in use. (H.C.Casserley)

PARKESTON QUAY

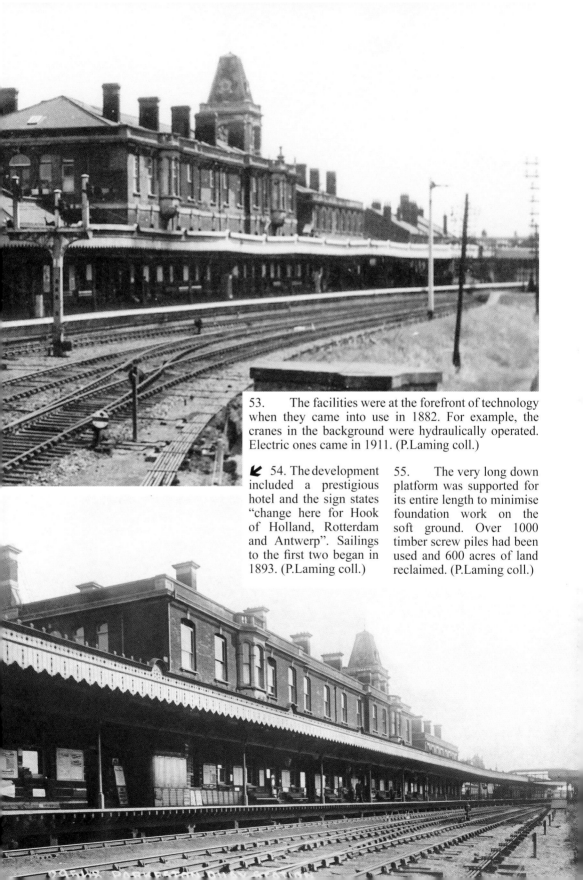

53.   The facilities were at the forefront of technology when they came into use in 1882. For example, the cranes in the background were hydraulically operated. Electric ones came in 1911. (P.Laming coll.)

↙ 54. The development included a prestigious hotel and the sign states "change here for Hook of Holland, Rotterdam and Antwerp". Sailings to the first two began in 1893. (P.Laming coll.)

55.   The very long down platform was supported for its entire length to minimise foundation work on the soft ground. Over 1000 timber screw piles had been used and 600 acres of land reclaimed. (P.Laming coll.)

VIIb.   The 1898 edition includes a quay capable of berthing seven ships. There are two signal boxes and a locomotive depot shown. There were five miles of siding at that time. The line lower left eventually served Harwich Refinery (Carless Solvents) and Yeoman Aggregates Tip Siding. The

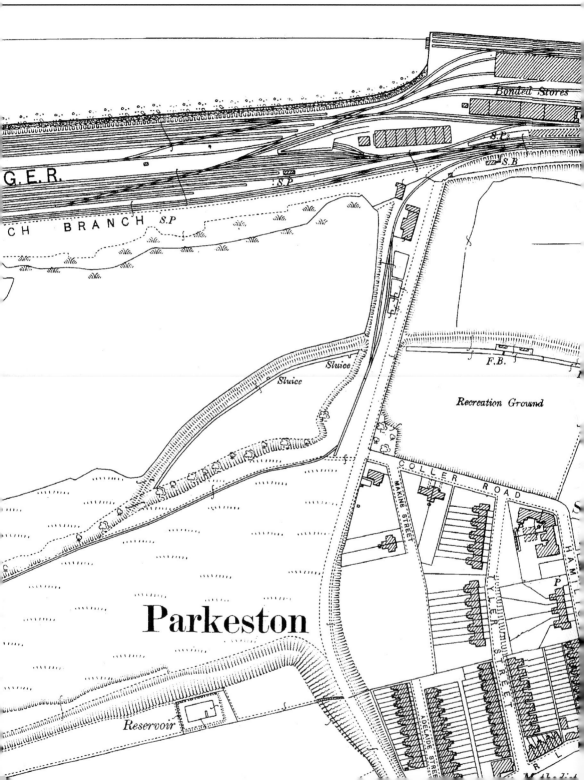

turntable was increased from 50 to 65ft in 1912. The village (lower) was built for GER employees. On the right are cattle sheds. Near the engine shed is Parkeston East Box. It had a 36-lever frame, which was in use from 1882 until 18th November 1973.

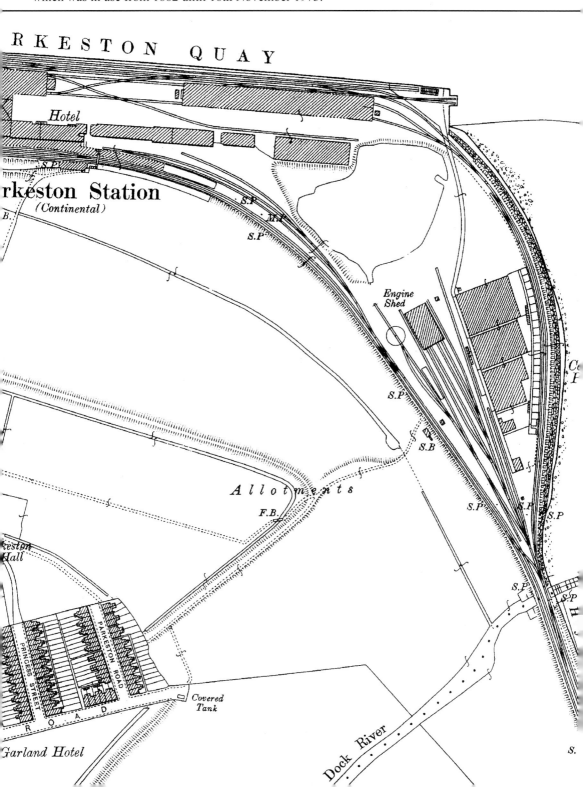

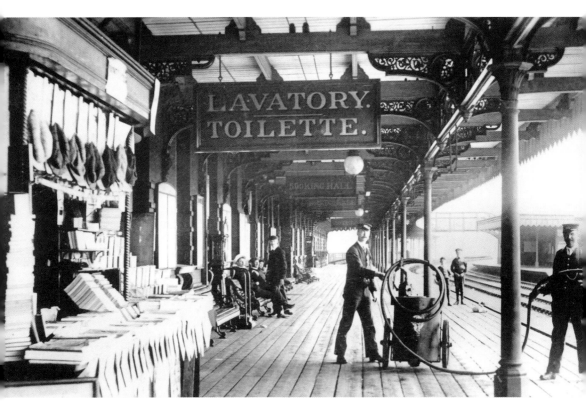

56.   The GER clearly did not wish any passenger to be inconvenienced. The staff have a fire pump, similar to those used to refill those tanks on the train concerned with sanitation. The ferries to Flushing began in 1927, so postcard humour was limited earlier. Amusing is the bookstall selling hats! (P.Laming coll.)

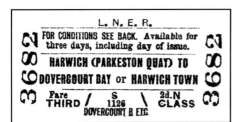

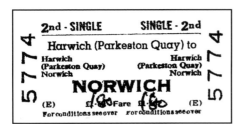

57.	The up platform (left) was much shorter than the down one. The bay platform (right) was used by the shuttle service to and from Harwich Town. The west end of the up platform is behind the porter on the right of the previous picture. (R.Laming coll.)

58.	An impressive boat train indeed, but sadly no details were recorded. The hotel tower is outstanding. (P.Laming coll.)

59. Parkeston handled a sizeable tonnage of goods traffic, the main items in 1938 being bacon and hams (nearly 60,000 tons), eggs (over 21,000 tons), butter, cheese and lard (17,000 tons), grain and flour, potatoes, slates and machinery. The capstans could be used during shunting operations. (P.Laming coll.)

60. LNER class B12 4-6-0 no. 8571 waits in the yard with a boat train, sometime in the 1930s. Note the white painted coach wheel rims to add status to the train. (R.R.Clow coll.)

HARWICH PARKESTON QUAY

61. The word "Harwich" was added to the name officially in 1934. Class J15 0-6-0 no. 65453 is leaving with a SR brake van on 9th January 1955. (R.R.Clow coll.)

→ 62. Parkeston was named after the chairman of the GER in the 1880s - Charles Henry Parkes. The name was always used for the engine shed, which was in use for steam until January 1960 and diesels until January 1967. It was coded 30F and had 33 locomotives in 1959. It is seen in 1911. Demolition came in 1967 to create a double-ended portal berth. (HMRS/R.R.Clow coll.)

→ 63. Departing with the 11.20am Harwich Town to Manningtree on 14th May 1956 is 0-6-2T no. 69552. This called at all stations and arrived at 11.53. There were around 1500 employed here at that period, many arriving by train. (H.C.Casserley)

← 64. Parkeston Quay West is in the background as no. D5524 creeps along with tankers containing Carless hydrocarbon solvents. Around 20,000 tons were despatched annually in the mid-1960s. (British Railways/ D.Brennand coll.)

↙ 65. The hotel closed in 1965 and became the port offices. The building is seen on 22nd July 1967, with a ship moored near the cranes. Local goods traffic had ceased on 1st May 1967. The tower has been shortened. (J.H.Meredith)

↓ 66. Seen on the same day is the transfer bus, hauled by Bedford SXT 77. Another is in the background; they were acceptable for short journeys. One crane was rated at 30 tons. (J.H.Meredith)

67.   The three tracks seen in picture ➔   68. By the 1970s, the view east was changing
63 had been reduced to two and part of   greatly. Freightliner traffic began on 21st May 1968.
the up platform widened with timber.   Passenger trains from here to Harwich Town used only
The old ramp is on the right.   the up track from January of that year.
(R.R.Clow coll.)   (Lens of Sutton coll.)

➔   69. More traffic was generated after the war as this became the port for BAOR (British
Army Of the Rhine), which occupied West Germany. The mid-1970s saw many alterations and
improvements, including platform realignment and new canopies. (Lens of Sutton coll.)

70.   Passengers were somewhat exposed during the alterations, but the original buildings remained standing. The train is the 13.00 Scandinavian Boat Train to Liverpool Street in about 1970. A new booking office was created in 1984. (Lens of Sutton coll.)

➔   71. The results of the alterations were recorded on 27th March 1976, by which time all the bullhead rail had gone. All three platforms could accommodate 13 coaches after the rebuilding. The next two photographs are from the same day. (R.F.Roberts/SLS coll.)

➔   72. Improved road access to the quays resulted in this unusual arrangement with wheeled barriers. Ro-Ro ships had been introduced here in 1964. Parkeston West Box is on the left, but it had been deprived of all its point rods and signal wires. A flyover for the road came later, but the crossing was retained as was this box. It was later replaced. (R.F.Roberts/SLS coll.)

73. The Freightliner Terminal eventually became the container terminal of Stena Sealink. Three parallel sidings were provided with a storage loop to the east. Initially the port was served by four Freightliner trains daily, these creating links with Stratford, Birmingham, Cardiff, Liverpool and Manchester. Later, additional services were provided to Leeds, Glasgow, Holyhead, Bristol, Southampton Millbrook, Willesden and Coatbridge in Scotland. 30,000 containers in 1968 increased to 100,000 in 1973, but a decline followed from 1986, when Felixstowe prevailed. (R.F.Roberts/ SLS coll.)

74. Parkeston Goods Junction Box was at the west end of the site and gave direct access to the sidings and also Quay West, the buildings of which are in the background in this 1984 panorama. The first signal box had 34 levers and functioned from about 1882 until 1934. This one had 56 and lasted until 1st December 1985. (D.C.Pearce)

75.   We are standing outside West Box in 1984 and can enjoy historic signalling, the 1965 boom gates and part of the massive yard. There were 12 freight sidings, 6 for carriages and, further north, there were 5 forming the car terminal, for their direct loading into ships over three ramps. The box had 50 levers and it was in use during 1934 to 1985. (D.C.Pearce)

76. The above name was applied to Parkeston Quay from 27th May 1995, but with PORT added. This was soon dropped. The 17.27 from Liverpool Street has just arrived on 30th July 2003, with a locomotive unusually at the front. This was because the driving compartment in the coach on the left was defective. Attached to it is Virgin Trains no. 86209 *City of Coventry*. (D.Pollock)

77. The new passenger terminal was completed in 1995 and it is seen from the west crossing, along with the new footbridge. No. 86218 *Planet* and coaching stock is stabled in platform 1 on 22nd February 1993, in readiness for a boat train working to Liverpool Street. An EMU was often sufficient as a boat train in 2011. The bridge nearest to us takes cars only, when the level crossing barriers are down. It is unidirectional, as traffic flows are during ship loading or unloading. (D.Pollock)

DOVERCOURT

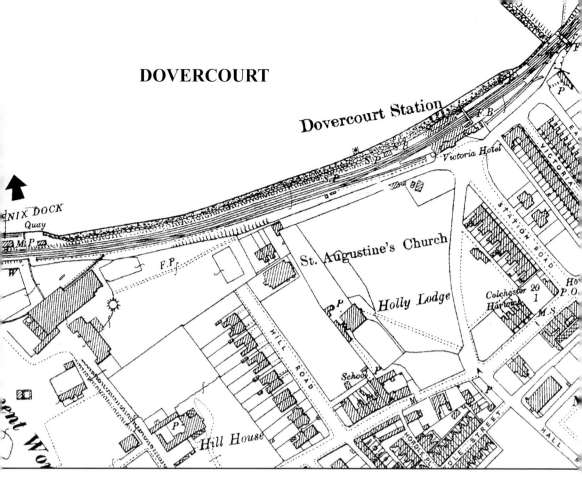

VIII.   The name was Dovercourt Bay from 1926 until 14th December 1972, since when it had its original name. The map is from 1898 and is at 20ins to 1 mile. An engine shed was in use west of the station from 1864 until 1883. The signal box had 25 levers and lasted from 1882 until 1st December 1985.

78.   The earliest view is from about 1898, when the covering of sleepers had not been totally banned. A second footbridge is visible, this being for public access to Bathside. (R.R.Clow coll.)

79.   Architectural detail was repeated at the station, but not the design. A bell was rung at some places prior to the arrival of a train, as many did not have a watch and public clocks were rare. (P.Laming coll.)

80.   A panorama from the public footbridge includes the shorter of the two sidings. The line on the right would appear to be part of a refuge siding. (HMRS/R.R.Clow)

81.   This is the view towards Harwich Town in the 1930s and includes the staff crossing in action. Presumably the milk churn is empty. (R.R.Clow coll.)

82. Local goods traffic ceased on 4th October 1965, the sidings being at opposite ends of the up platform. Seen in the 1960s are LNER lamp globes and evidence of bidirectional signalling. The crossover was taken out of use on 1st December 1985. (Lens of Sutton coll.)

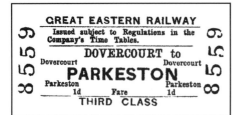

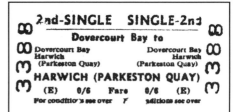

83.   Viewed in the same period, the south facade had received a notable modification, maybe as a result of storm damage. The red telephone box was not to survive, neither was the word BAY. (Lens of Sutton coll.)

84.   The first day of electric operation was recorded as no. 312783 calls on 12th May 1986. The up platform has been lengthened to take eight cars. The down one has vanished, as that line had become freight only on 13th January 1968. The shore on the right has subsequently been reclaimed for the new A120 alignment. (Colour-Rail.com)

85. When photographed on 17th June 1997, the historic building was subject to major renovation work. The gates on the left had been of value during the era of parcel traffic. (B.W.L.Brooksbank)

EAST OF DOVERCOURT

86. No. 312715 has just left Harwich Town at 13.15 on 22nd February 2003 and near the rear of the train can be seen the points to Bank Siding. Out of view is Alexandra Road level crossing, which passes over all three tracks. The crossing received manually controlled barriers on 12th December 1965. Beyond that is a crossover, which links the running line with the long siding from Harwich International, which was still in place in 2011 although heavily overgrown. (D.Pollock)

HARWICH TOWN

IX. The word TOWN was added on 1st March 1883. The Rotterdam Boat Express still ran on to New Pier as late as 1877. The map is the 1898 edition and it includes tracks on to both piers. The turntable was 42ft in length.

HARBOUR

PIER

Crane

Crane

Pier Hotel

Great Eastern Hotel

NEW PIER

Goods Shed

Crane

Crane

Crane

Trinity Stores

Cattle Pen

Timber Yard

Quay

Gas Works

Quay

Timber Yard

Anchot Hotel

Hotel

Goods Shed

L.B

St Nicholas's Church

School

B.S.W.A.D. NO.12

NO.13

B.S.W.A.D. NO.14

B.S.W.A.D. NO.15

B.S.W.A.D. NO.16

B.S.W.A.D. NO.17

WELLINGTON ROAD

Trinity Cottages

High Lighthouse (Disused)

Life Boat

OU

THE GREEN

D.Fn

Terminus

S.P.

School

R. C. Church

B.S.W.A.D. NO.19

B.S.W.A.D. NO.20

PEPYS ST

ALBEMARLE STREET

COKE STREET

MARIA STREET

VANSITTART STREET

Macdonough Cottages

S.B.

FERNLEA ROAD

Public Hall

Pumping

LAS

WICH WARD

OUTER PART OF TOW
WESTWARD
B.S

Tower Hill

87.   This is the 1854 terminus, which closed on 1st December 1865. It was at the north end of George Street; the other side of the station was close to the quay, and therefore convenient for ship access. However, it stood on the route of the line to the new pier and was thus demolished. It was burnt down. (R.R.Clow coll.)

88.   The end of the line is on the right and on it is an ECR wagon carrying a cart. Two dry docks are shown at the top of the map. (R.R.Clow coll.)

89.   An early motor bus passes the GER hotel, while a horse and cart stands outside the Commercial. This would have accommodated commercial travellers, now known as reps. The location is at the top of the map. (P.Laming coll.)

90.   We are looking north from the bottom edge of the map, with the sewage pump house on the right, a pony and trap on the level crossing and the terminal platforms in the distance. The signal box retained its original name and was in use from 1882 until 1st December 1985. It had 50 levers. (HMRS/R.R.Clow coll.)

91.   Export items were derailed in the goods yard, while being shunted in the late 1950s by class J15 0-6-0 no. 65458. Ferry vans were noted for their garden shed appearance. (R.R.Clow coll.)

92.   Three platforms were still in use on 5th August 1959 when a Cravens DMU was photographed at No. 1 and about to depart for Manningtree at 13.05. On the right is the shuttle service to Parkeston Quay. (R.R.Clow coll.)

93.   Devoid of cats whiskers, another Cravens unit was to be seen on 4th September 1981, while a traffic jam waits to be exported and weeds adorn the neglected platform. (B.Morrison)

94.	Standing at platform 3 is a Matix Industrie permanent way ultrasonic scanning train. The goods yard closed to local traffic on 4th October 1965. (R.F.Roberts/SLS coll.)

95.	The approach was uncluttered when photographed on 3rd May 1986, apart from trees occluding unused rooms on the left. Centre is a drinking fountain, which has been preserved by a local group. (J .M.Rickard/Colour-Rail.com)

96.   Operationally, the line had been single from Parkeston Quay since January 1968, thus only one wire was needed and only platform 1 was upgraded. It could accommodate eight coaches. The goods shed was still standing in 2011, but the line to the pier had been built over.
(R.F.Roberts/SLS coll.)

97.   The end of the line on 17th June 1997 was a "sight" of mixed sentiments. The joys of modernisation were accompanied by the sadness of lost freight opportunities. On the right is one of two circular electric signals used to control trains loading the ships. It is outlined against the sky and both were still standing in 2011. (B.W.L.Brooksbank)

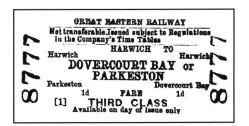

HARWICH PIER

98.   This train ferry berth was built in 1924, using parts brought from Southampton, where ships had worked to and from France during World War I. A similar service had operated from Richborough in Kent and some train ferries came from there. This view is from the bridge of a ship. (P.Laming coll.)

99.   The ships could carry 50 wagons of ten-ton capacity each. This view shows the link span in LNER days, with a class B12 on the right. The traffic eventually grew dramatically from 82,638 tons in 1948 to 234,568 in 1958 and 380,025 in 1968. It later dropped, due to the export of cars by other means. (R.R.Clow coll.)

100. The only train ferry to carry passengers was on the Dover-Dunkirk route. These French Wagon Lits cars are being unloaded in 1924 for the British Empire Exhibition. The Sealink train-ferry between Harwich and Zeebrugge was discontinued on 30th January 1987 and rail traffic ceased on the pier. (R.R.Clow coll.)

101. Successive railway operators have run the ferry service to Felixstowe and Vosper built this vessel in Portsmouth for the GER in 1914. The MV *Epping* is seen on 15th December 1962. Private enterprise has operated the service since railway privatisation. (J.H.Meredith)

2. Hadleigh Branch
BENTLEY

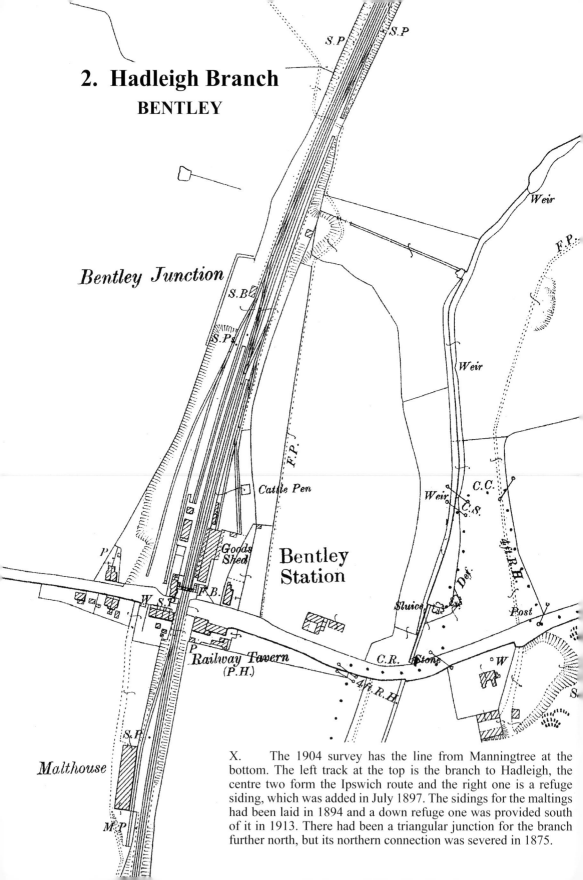

Bentley Junction

S.B.

S.P.

S.P.

F.P.

Weir

F.P.

Weir

Weir

C.C.

C.S.

Cattle Pen

4 ft. R.H.

Goods Shed

P.

Def.

Bentley Station

Sluice

Post

W.S.P.

F.B.

C.R.

Stone

W

Railway Tavern
(P.H.)

4 ft. R.H.

S.P.

Malthouse

M.P.

X.   The 1904 survey has the line from Manningtree at the bottom. The left track at the top is the branch to Hadleigh, the centre two form the Ipswich route and the right one is a refuge siding, which was added in July 1897. The sidings for the maltings had been laid in 1894 and a down refuge one was provided south of it in 1913. There had been a triangular junction for the branch further north, but its northern connection was severed in 1875.

102. The down platform was provided with this modest building and beyond it stands a train from Hadleigh. There are five oil lamps, one with a ladder. (P.Laming coll.)

BENTLEY and HADLEIGH.—Great Eastern.												Arrives at 8 15 aft. on Sats.								
	mrn	mrn	mrn	aft		aft	Tues. only.	aft	Sats. only.	aft	**Up.**	mrn	mrn	aft		aft	r.	aft	Tues. only.	aft	Sats. only.	aft
Liverpool Street, LONDON 236 dep.	....	6 47	1145	2 25		3 32		3 32		5 30	Hadleigh ....dep.	7 55	9 14	1 10	2 58		5 35		6 50		6 56
Bentley ......dep.	8 33	9 43	1 48	5 7		6 20		6 27		7 23	Raydon Wood	8 0	9 19	1 15	3 3		5 42		6 55		7 1
Capel	8 40	9 49	1 54	5 13		6 26		6 33		7 29	Capel	8 6	9 26	1 22	3 10		5 52		7 2		7 8
Raydon Wood	8 49	9 56	2 1	5 20		6 33		6 40		7 36	Bentley 240, 236	8 12	9 32	1 28	3 16		6 0		7 7		7 14
Hadleigh ....arr.	8 56	10 2	2 7	5 26		6 39		6 46		7 42	LONDON 240 arr.	1026	....	3 33								

January 1901

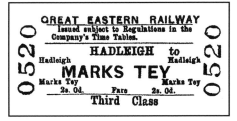
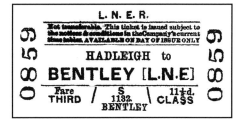

103.   We can enjoy two fine photographs from 12th September 1911. This features a train bound for Hadleigh, headed by a class E22 0-6-0. The bay could take five coaches. (Windwood/NRM)

104.   This is a panorama from the signal post platform seen in the previous picture and was recorded on the same day. The Hadleigh branch is on the left and a few passenger trains from it reversed here to Ipswich and vice versa. The signal box had 33 levers and was in use until 1913. It was called Hadleigh Junction Box, but the station was termed Bentley Junction in 1849-78. (Windwood/NRM)

Views of the main buildings at this station can be found in the companion album *Shenfield to Ipswich*.

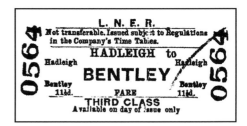

105.	A broad view in 1955 includes the longer shelter on the up platform and only one signal on the down side. The bay platform was taken out of use on 29th February 1932 and the others followed on 7th November 1966. The 1913 signal box is in the distance. It was called Bentley Junction. It had 50 levers and was in use until 29th June 1975. (Stations UK)

106.	Class J17 no. 65578 rests on 2nd August 1956, while we gain a glimpse of the footbridge, which had been moved here from Parkeston Quay in 1894. All the station buildings had been demolished by 1984. (G.W.Powell/Colour-Rail.com)

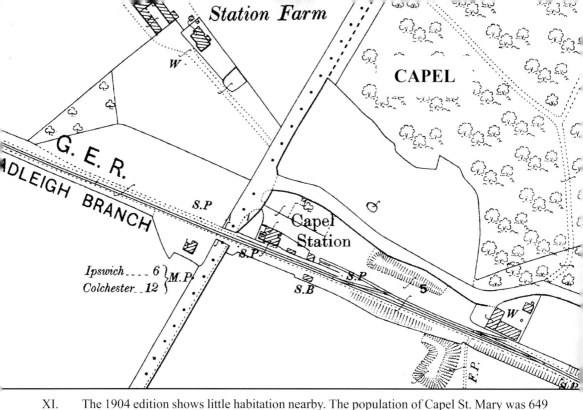

XI.   The 1904 edition shows little habitation nearby. The population of Capel St. Mary was 649 in 1851 and only 504 in 1931. We have now climbed to 150ft above sea level. There was a 20-lever signal box from 1891 until 1923.

107.   Flambouyant styling was employed at vast cost, this being the view from the road. Severe problems on the A12 due to the level crossing resulted in traffic lights being installed in 1962. These enabled train crews to close the gates without confrontations. (Stations UK)

108.   Built to high standards, the structure was still in reasonable condition when photographed in 1955. A ground frame was in use from 1923. Note that fire buckets still hang on the wall of the gents. (Stations UK)

109.   An extra siding was added in 1913 and both are seen from a special train on 30th September 1956. The goods yard closed on 13th July 1964. There is no trace now, as the site is under the A12. (R.M.Casserley)

RAYDON WOOD

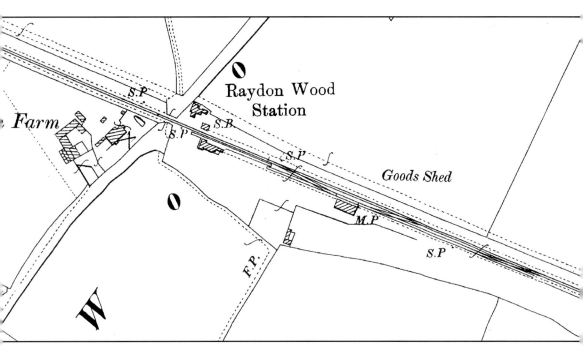

XII.   The name was simply Raydon until 1st October 1895 and the station is seen on the 1904 edition. Capel's goods yard and this one were both busy during World War II, as the USAF had a base nearby.

110.   There had been a 20-lever signal box on the right until April 1923, but ground frames sufficed thereafter. One is right of centre. Tickets were issued on the train from 1922. Examples are 4248 in 1923 and 1985 in 1928. (P.Laming coll.)

111.   This picture was taken minutes after no. 109 and it includes two oil lamps intact, 24 years after the last passenger was helped by them. (R.M.Casserley)

112.   Seen in the 1950s, the station was never busy. There were 555 local residents in 1851 and only 435 in 1931. The goods yard closed on 16th April 1965. (W.A.Camwell/SLS coll.)

HADLEIGH

XIII.   The 1926 issue shows a layout which seems to have remained almost unchanged. The hydraulic ram was a water operated water pump. The signal box is to the left of it and its 24-lever frame was in use from 1892 until 27th September 1932. There were 3716 residents in the town in 1851 and 2951 in 1931.

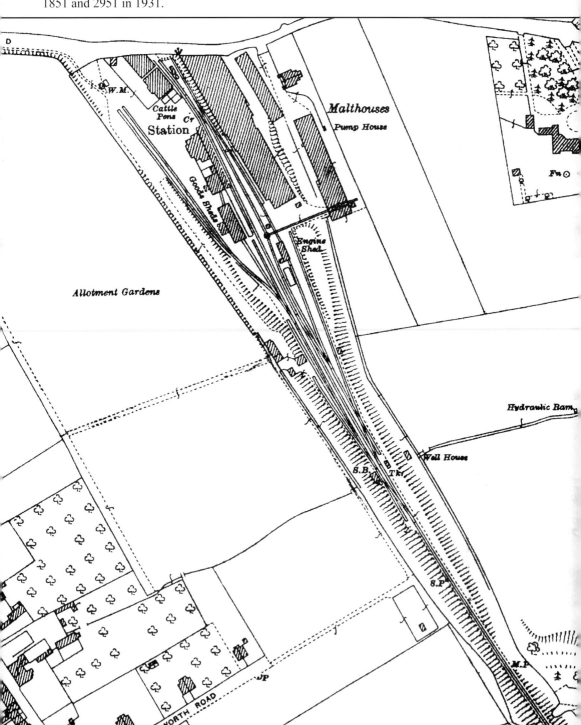

113.   An 0-6-0T arrives in 1906 and shelters under the overall roof, common in the early years of railways. It would run round, using one of the tracks near the malthouse. (R.G.Pratt)

114.   The previous picture was taken near the left of this one, which includes the goods shed on the right. Tickets issued numbered 14,447 in 1923, but only 5086 in 1928. (P.Laming coll.)

115.   It is 12th September 1911 and sheeted hay waits on the left, but the old goods shed is largely obscured by the light-coloured new one. Coaches wait at the platform and locomotive coal is stacked near the engine shed, which closed on 29th February 1932. (Windwood/NRM)

116.   A closer view in 1949 features the wagon turntable and shows that its siding had been curtailed by buffer stops. The blocks in the foreground are to arrest any errant wagons from the maltings. The overall roof had gone at an early date. (P.Paye coll.)

↓ 117. The replacement platform canopy retained its gas lights 21 years after passenger traffic had ceased. The van is standing near the crane. (Stations UK)

← 118. More of the crane is seen on 9th June 1956 when a Railway Enthusiasts Club special called, hauled by class J15 0-6-0 no. 65459. The REC ran another on 30th September 1956, behind 2-4-0 no. 62797.
(R.M.Casserley)

↙ 119. Photographed in the same month are the splendid coupled chimney stacks and the unusual window with frame and arch in stone.
(R.M.Casserley)

↓ 120. Diesel haulage came to the branch in 1960 and no. D5544 was recorded on 20th April 1962. This locomotive had hauled a special, organised by the Ramblers Association that day, the last ever to carry rural branch admirers here.
(Colour-Rail.com)

Middleton Press

EVOLVING THE ULTIMATE RAIL ENCYCLOPEDIA

Easebourne Lane, Midhurst, West Sussex.
GU29 9AZ   Tel:01730 813169

www.middletonpress.co.uk   email:info@middletonpress.co.uk
A-978 0 906520 B- 978 1 873793 C- 978 1 901706 D-978 1 904474
E - 978 1 906008   F - 978 1 908174

All titles listed below were in print at time of publication - please check current availability by looking at our
website - *www.middletonpress.co.uk* or by requesting a Brochure which includes our
LATEST RAILWAY TITLES also our TRAMWAY, TROLLEYBUS, MILITARY and WATERWAYS series

A
Abergavenny to Merthyr C 91 8
Abertillery and Ebbw Vale Lines D 84 5
Aberystwyth to Carmarthen E 90 1
Allhallows - Branch Line to A 62 8
Alton - Branch Lines to A 11 6
Andover to Southampton A 82 6
Ascot - Branch Lines around A 64 2
Ashburton - Branch Line to B 95 4
Ashford - Steam to Eurostar B 67 1
Ashford to Dover A 48 2
Austrian Narrow Gauge D 04 3
Avonmouth - BL around D 42 5
Aylesbury to Rugby D 91 3

B
Baker Street to Uxbridge D 90 6
Bala to Llandudno E 87 1
Banbury to Birmingham D 27 2
Banbury to Cheltenham E 63 5
Bangor to Portmadoc E 72 7
Barking to Southend C 80 2
Barmouth to Pwllheli E 53 6
Barry - Branch Lines around D 50 0
Bath Green Park to Bristol C 36 9
Bath to Evercreech Junction A 60 4
Beamish 40 years on rails E94 9
Bedford to Wellingborough D 31 9
Birmingham to Wolverhampton E 25 3
Bletchley to Cambridge D 94 4
Bletchley to Rugby E 07 9
Bodmin - Branch Lines around B 83 1
Bournemouth to Evercreech Jn A 46 8
Bournemouth to Weymouth A 57 4
Brecon to Neath D 43 2
Brecon to Newport D 16 6
Brecon to Newtown E 06 2
Brighton to Eastbourne A 16 1
Brighton to Worthing A 03 1
Bromley South to Rochester B 23 7
Bromsgrove to Birmingham D 87 6
Bromsgrove to Gloucester D 73 9
Brunel - A railtour of his achievements D 74 6
Bude - Branch Line to B 29 9
Burnham to Evercreech Junction B 68 0

C
Cambridge to Ely D 55 5
Canterbury - Branch Lines around B 58 9
Cardiff to Dowlais (Cae Harris) E 47 5
Cardiff to Pontypridd E 95 6
Cardiff to Swansea E 42 0
Carlisle to Hawick E 85 7
Carmarthen to Fishguard E 66 6
Caterham & Tattenham Corner B 25 1
Central & Southern Spain NG E 91 8
Chard and Yeovil - BLs around C 30 7
Charing Cross to Dartford A 75 8
Charing Cross to Orpington A 96 3
Cheddar - Branch Line to B 90 9
Cheltenham to Andover C 43 7
Cheltenham to Redditch D 81 4
Chester to Rhyl E 93 2
Chichester to Portsmouth A 14 7
Clapham Junction to Beckenham Jn B 36 7
Cleobury Mortimer - BLs around E 18 5
Clevedon & Portishead - BLs to D 18 0
Colonel Stephens - His Empire D 62 3
Consett to South Shields E 57 4
Cornwall Narrow Gauge D 56 2
Corris and Vale of Rheidol E 65 9
Craven Arms to Llandeilo E 35 2
Craven Arms to Wellington E 33 8
Crawley to Littlehampton A 34 5
Cromer - Branch Lines around C 26 0
Croydon to East Grinstead B 48 0
Crystal Palace and Catford Loop B 87 1
Cyprus Narrow Gauge E 13 0

D
Darlington - Leamside - Newcastle E 28 4
Darlington to Newcastle D 98 2
Dartford to Sittingbourne B 34 3
Derwent Valley - Branch Line to the D 06 7
Devon Narrow Gauge E 09 3
Didcot to Banbury D 02 9

Didcot to Swindon C 84 0
Didcot to Winchester C 13 0
Dorset & Somerset Narrow Gauge D 76 0
Douglas - Laxey - Ramsey E 75 8
Douglas to Peel C 88 8
Douglas to Port Erin C 55 0
Douglas to Ramsey D 39 5
Dover to Ramsgate A 78 9
Dublin Northwards in the 1950s E 31 4
Dunstable - Branch Lines to E 27 7

E
Ealing to Slough C 42 0
East Cornwall Mineral Railways D 22 7
East Croydon to Three Bridges A 53 6
Eastern Spain Narrow Gauge E 56 7
East Grinstead - Branch Lines to A 07 9
East London - Branch Lines of C 44 4
East London Line B 80 0
East of Norwich - Branch Lines E 69 7
Effingham Junction - BLs around A 74 1
Ely to Norwich C 90 1
Enfield Town & Palace Gates - BL to D 32 6
Epsom to Horsham A 30 7
Eritrean Narrow Gauge E 38 3
Euston to Harrow & Wealdstone C 89 5
Exeter to Barnstaple B 15 2
Exeter to Newton Abbot C 49 9
Exeter to Tavistock B 69 5
Exmouth - Branch Lines to B 00 8

F
Fairford - Branch Line to A 52 9
Falmouth, Helston & St. Ives - BL to C 74 1
Fareham to Salisbury A 67 3
Faversham to Dover B 05 3
Felixstowe & Aldeburgh - BL to D 20 3
Fenchurch Street to Barking C 20 8
Festiniog - 50 yrs of enterprise C 83 3
Festiniog 1946-55 E 01 7
Festiniog in the Fifties B 68 8
Festiniog in the Sixties B 91 6
Finsbury Park to Alexandra Palace C 02 8
Frome to Bristol B 77 0

G
Gloucester to Bristol D 35 7
Gloucester to Cardiff D 66 1
Gosport - Branch Lines around A 36 9
Greece Narrow Gauge D 72 2

H
Hampshire Narrow Gauge D 36 4
Harrow to Watford D 14 2
Harwich & Hadleigh - Branch Lines to F 02 4
Hastings to Ashford A 37 6
Hawkhurst - Branch Line to A 66 6
Hayling - Branch Line to A 12 3
Hay-on-Wye - Branch Lines around D 92 0
Haywards Heath to Seaford A 28 4
Hemel Hempstead - Branch Lines to D 88 3
Henley, Windsor & Marlow - BL to C77 2
Hereford to Newport D 54 8
Hertford and Hatfield - BLs around E 58 1 6
Hertford Loop E 71 0
Hexham to Carlisle D 75 3
Hitchin to Peterborough D 07 4
Holborn Viaduct to Lewisham A 81 9
Horsham - Branch Lines to A 02 4
Huntingdon - Branch Line to A 93 2

I
Ilford to Shenfield C 97 0
Ilfracombe - Branch Line to B 21 3
Industrial Rlys of the South East A 09 3
Ipswich to Saxmundham C 41 3
Isle of Wight Lines - 50 yrs C 12 3

K
Kent Narrow Gauge C 45 1
Kidderminster to Shrewsbury E 10 9
Kingsbridge - Branch Line to C 98 7
Kings Cross to Potters Bar E 62 8
Kingston & Hounslow Loops A 83 3
Kingswear - Branch Line to C 17 8

L
Lambourn - Branch Line to C 70 3
Launceston & Princetown - BL to C 19 2

Lewisham to Dartford A 92 5
Lines around Wimbledon B 75 6
Liverpool Street to Chingford D 01 2
Liverpool Street to Ilford C 34 5
Llandeilo to Swansea E 46 8
London Bridge to Addiscombe B 20 6
London Bridge to East Croydon A 58 1
Longmoor - Branch Lines to A 41 3
Looe - Branch Line to C 22 2
Lowestoft - Branch Lines around E 40 6
Ludlow to Hereford E 14 7
Lydney - Branch Lines around E 26 0
Lyme Regis - Branch Line to A 45 1
Lynton - Branch Line to B 04 6

M
Machynlleth to Barmouth E 54 3
March - Branch Lines around B 09 1
Marylebone to Rickmansworth D 49 4
Melton Constable to Yarmouth Beach E 03 1
Midhurst - Branch Lines of E 78 9
Mitcham Junction Lines B 01 5
Mitchell & company C 59 8
Monmouth - Branch Lines to E 20 8
Monmouthshire Eastern Valleys D 71 5
Moretonhampstead - BL to C 27 7
Moreton-in-Marsh to Worcester D 26 5
Mountain Ash to Neath D 80 7

N
Newbury to Westbury C 66 6
Newcastle to Hexham D 69 2
Newport (IOW) - Branch Lines to A 26 0
Newquay - Branch Lines to C 71 0
Newton Abbot to Plymouth C 60 4
Newtown to Aberystwyth E 41 3
North East German Narrow Gauge D 44 9
Northern France Narrow Gauge C 75 8
Northern Spain Narrow Gauge E 83 3
North London Line B 94 7
North Woolwich - BLs around C 65 9

O
Ongar - Branch Line to E 05 5
Oswestry - Branch Lines around E 60 4
Oswestry to Whitchurch E 81 9
Oxford to Bletchley D 57 9
Oxford to Moreton-in-Marsh D 15 9

P
Paddington to Ealing C 37 6
Paddington to Princes Risborough C 81 9
Padstow - Branch Line to B 54 1
Peterborough to Kings Lynn E 32 1
Plymouth - BLs around B 98 5
Plymouth to St. Austell C 63 5
Pontypool to Mountain Ash D 65 4
Pontypridd to Port Talbot E 86 4
Porthmadog 1954-94 - BL around B 31 2
Portmadoc 1923-46 - BL around B 13 8
Portsmouth to Southampton A 31 4
Portugal Narrow Gauge E 67 3
Potters Bar to Cambridge D 70 8
Princes Risborough - Branch Lines to D 05 0
Princes Risborough to Banbury C 85 7

R
Reading to Basingstoke B 27 5
Reading to Didcot C 79 6
Reading to Guildford A 47 5
Redhill to Ashford A 73 4
Return to Blaenau 1970-82 C 64 2
Rhymney and New Tredegar Lines E 48 2
Rickmansworth to Aylesbury D 61 6
Romania & Bulgaria Narrow Gauge E 23 9
Romneyrail C 32 1
Ross-on-Wye - Branch Lines around E 30 7
Ruabon to Barmouth E 84 0
Rugby to Birmingham E 37 6
Ryde to Ventnor A 19 2

S
Salisbury to Westbury B 39 8
Saxmundham to Yarmouth C 69 7
Saxony Narrow Gauge D 47 0
Seaton & Sidmouth - Branch Lines to A 95 6
Selsey - Branch Line to A 04 8
Sheerness - Branch Line to B 16 2

Shenfield to Ipswich E 96 3
Shrewsbury - Branch Line to A 86 4
Shrewsbury to Chester E 70 3
Shrewsbury to Ludlow E 21 5
Shrewsbury to Newtown E 29 1
Sierra Leone Narrow Gauge D 28 9
Sirhowy Valley Line E 12 3
Sittingbourne to Ramsgate A 90 1
Slough to Newbury C 56 7
South African Two-foot gauge E 51 2
Southampton to Bournemouth A 42
Southend & Southminster - B Ls to E
Southern France Narrow Gauge C 47
South London Line B 46 6
Southwold - Branch Line to A 15 4
Spalding - Branch Lines around E 52
St Albans to Bedford D 08 1
St. Austell to Penzance C 67 3
Steaming through the Isle of Wight A
Steaming through West Hants A 69
Stourbridge to Wolverhampton E 16
St. Pancras to Barking D 68 5
St. Pancras to Folkestone E 88 8
St. Pancras to St. Albans C 78 9
Stratford-upon-Avon to Birmingham
Stratford-upon-Avon to Cheltenham
Surrey Narrow Gauge C 87 1
Sussex Narrow Gauge C 68 0
Swanley to Ashford B 45 9
Swansea to Carmarthen E 59 8
Swindon to Bristol C 96 3
Swindon to Gloucester D 46 3
Swindon to Newport D 30 2
Swiss Narrow Gauge C 94 9

T
Talyllyn 60 E 98 7
Taunton to Barnstaple B 60 2
Taunton to Exeter C 82 6
Tavistock to Plymouth B 88 6
Tenterden - Branch Line to A 21 5
Three Bridges to Brighton A 35 2
Tilbury Loop C 86 4
Tiverton - Branch Lines around C 62
Tivetshall to Beccles D 41 8
Tonbridge to Hastings A 44 4
Torrington - Branch Lines to B 37 4
Towcester - Branch Lines around E
Tunbridge Wells - Branch Lines to A

U
Upwell - Branch Line to B 64 0

V
Victoria to Bromley South A 98 7
Vivarais Revisited E 08 6

W
Wantage - Branch Line to D 25 8
Wareham to Swanage - 50 yrs D 09
Waterloo to Windsor A 54 3
Waterloo to Woking A 38 3
Watford to Leighton Buzzard D 45 6
Welshpool to Llanfair E 49 9
Wenford Bridge to Fowey C 09 3
Westbury to Bath B 55 8
Westbury to Taunton C 76 5
West Cornwall Mineral Railways D 2
West Croydon to Epsom B 08 4
West German Narrow Gauge D 93 7
West London - Branch Lines of C 50
West London Line B 84 8
West Wiltshire - Branch Lines of D 1
Weymouth - Branch Lines around A
Willesden Junction to Richmond B 7
Wimbledon to Beckenham C 58 1
Wimbledon to Epsom B 62 6
Wimborne - Branch Lines around A
Wisbech 1800-1901 C 93 2
Wisbech - Branch Lines around E 1
Witham & Kelvedon - BLs around E
Woking to Alton A 59 8
Woking to Portsmouth A 25 3
Woking to Southampton A 55 0
Wolverhampton to Shrewsbury E 44
Worcester to Birmingham D 97 5
Worcester to Hereford D 38 8
Worthing to Chichester A 06 2

Y
Yeovil - 50 yrs change C 38 3
Yeovil to Dorchester A 76 5
Yeovil to Exeter A 91 8